WHAT YOU SEE IS NOT ALWAYS WHAT YOU GET

In 2014, artist Yunuene incorporated Augmented Reality into one of her paintings as a way to experiment with new technologies.

Since then, she has been using it as a way to deepen the story behind each piece, never imagining that her project would gain such international acclaim.

She often infuses humor and strong social messages into her work, taking full advantage of the marriage of traditional media and technology.

Her deconstructive technique reflects a kaleidoscopic view of the world that reveals its geometric essence.

She uses cultural and biographical elements like different tiles in a mosaic to compose a final vision charged with vibrant chromatic energy.

Yunuene lives and works in Mexico City.
Art Party is her first book.

Art Party

AUGMENTED REALITY ART

TO ENJOY THE AUGMENTED REALITY IN THIS BOOK
INSTALL **YUNUENE ART** APP

YOU CAN SCAN THE QR CODE ABOVE TO FIND IT

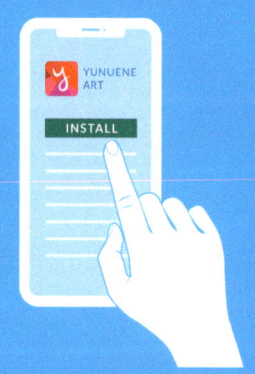

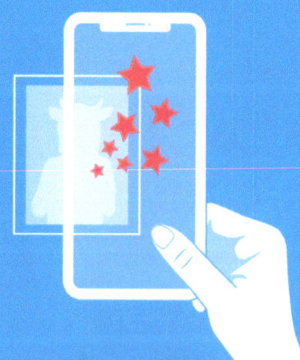

INSTALL
YUNUENE ART

START THE APP
**POINT IT TOWARDS
THE ART**

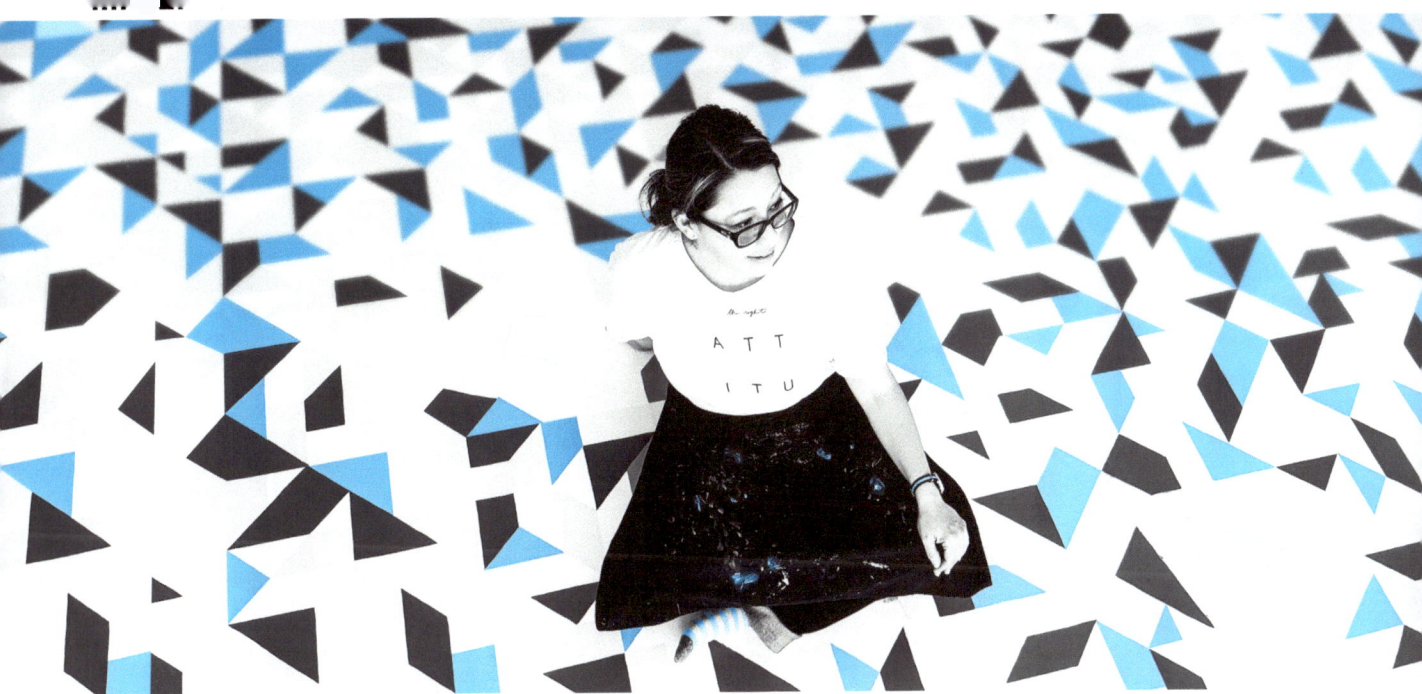

Hi! I'm Yunuene, seen here sitting on top of one of my installations.
I invite you to embark on a colorful journey to personal experiences represented through art. But first, let's go back to where it all began.

I've spent most of my life in Mexico City influenced by its culture and beauty. My mother, an interior decorator and teacher, shared with me her passion for all things artistic. When I was twelve, Vincent Van Gogh was my first love. Many years later I majored in Graphic Design.

In 1998, fresh out of college, I worked at an advertising agency using a computer the size of a fridge to display virtual graphics on live TV. Sometimes I used it to create artistic stuff (please don't tell my boss).
In those days technology felt like magic!
I started painting with traditional media in 2010, gradually evolving to develop my style and technique.

Sixteen years after my first job, modern cellphones became capable of achieving the same feats as those old massive computers. I realized virtual graphics could finally be incorporated into my work. With the help of my husband, a systems engineer, we developed an app to view the paintings.
In November 2014 "The Funeral", my first painting with Augmented Reality, was exhibited at the Autonoma UNAM Gallery. The reaction was immediate! It was so well-received that the word spread quickly. One year later I was presenting a solo art show in New York City.

Today, my work has been exhibited all over the world, with a growing portfolio of more than 70 pieces of art enhanced with AR. It has been one incredible ride! In this book you will experience three of my most beloved art collections.
I hope you enjoy them as much as I enjoyed creating them.

Prepare your mobile device and get ready to be surprised!

MOTHERHOOD
COLLECTION

Motherhood has been very challenging for me. Sometimes I feel like I'm raising creatures from a different species. In this series, I re-imagine children as cute but bizarre animals in absurd and common situations, trying to convey a more realistic and less romantic concept of what it means to be a mother.

BRAIN FREEZE

2018 / Oil on Canvas / 70x90 cm

Once you become a mother, many times you feel helpless. Your brain freezes, and the absurd becomes real. Like this cow eating an ice cream.

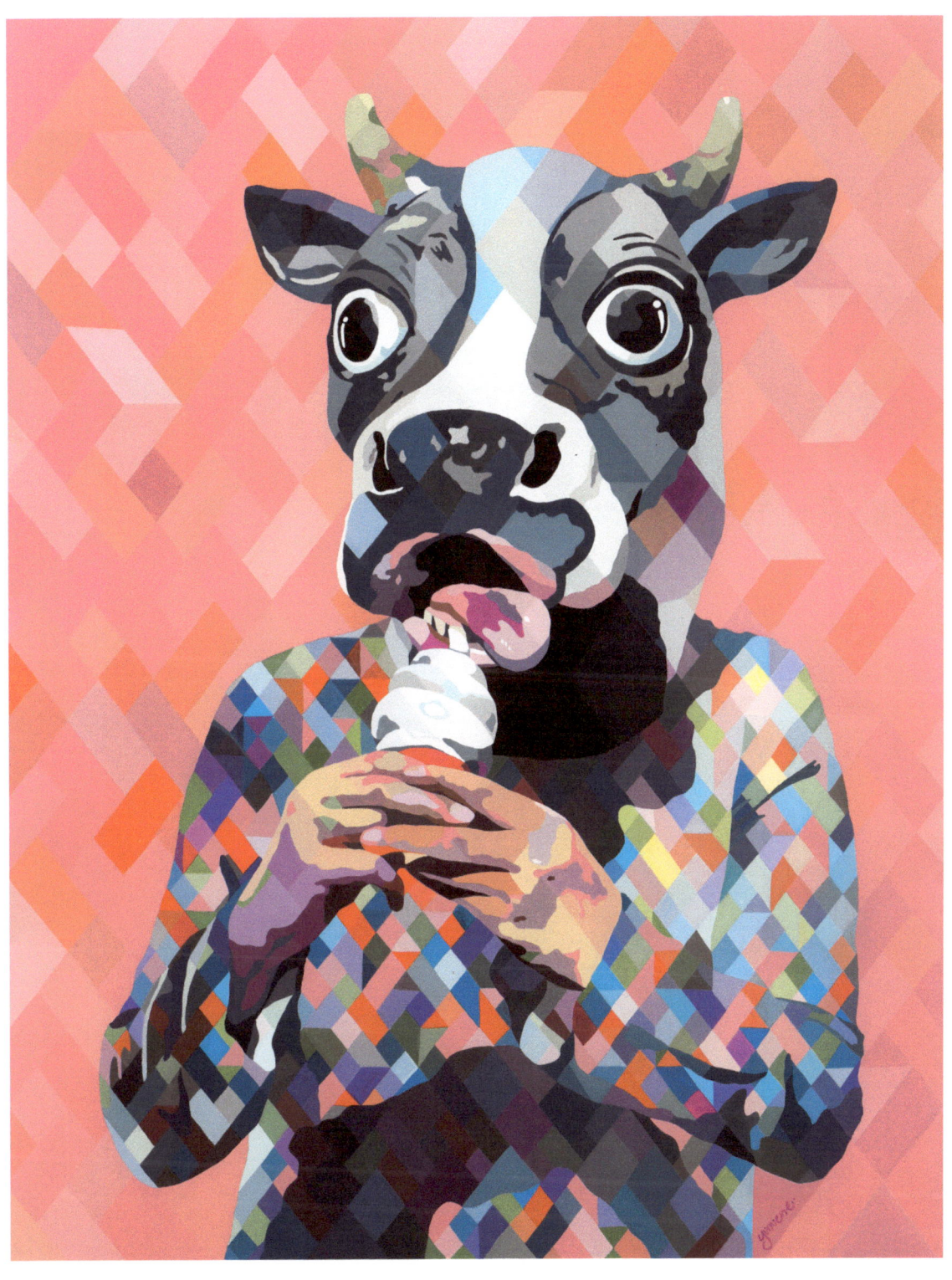

ROCINANTE

2018 / Oil on Canvas / 100x150 cm

Maternity is a trip filled with adventures: fun, crazy and sometimes quite challenging.

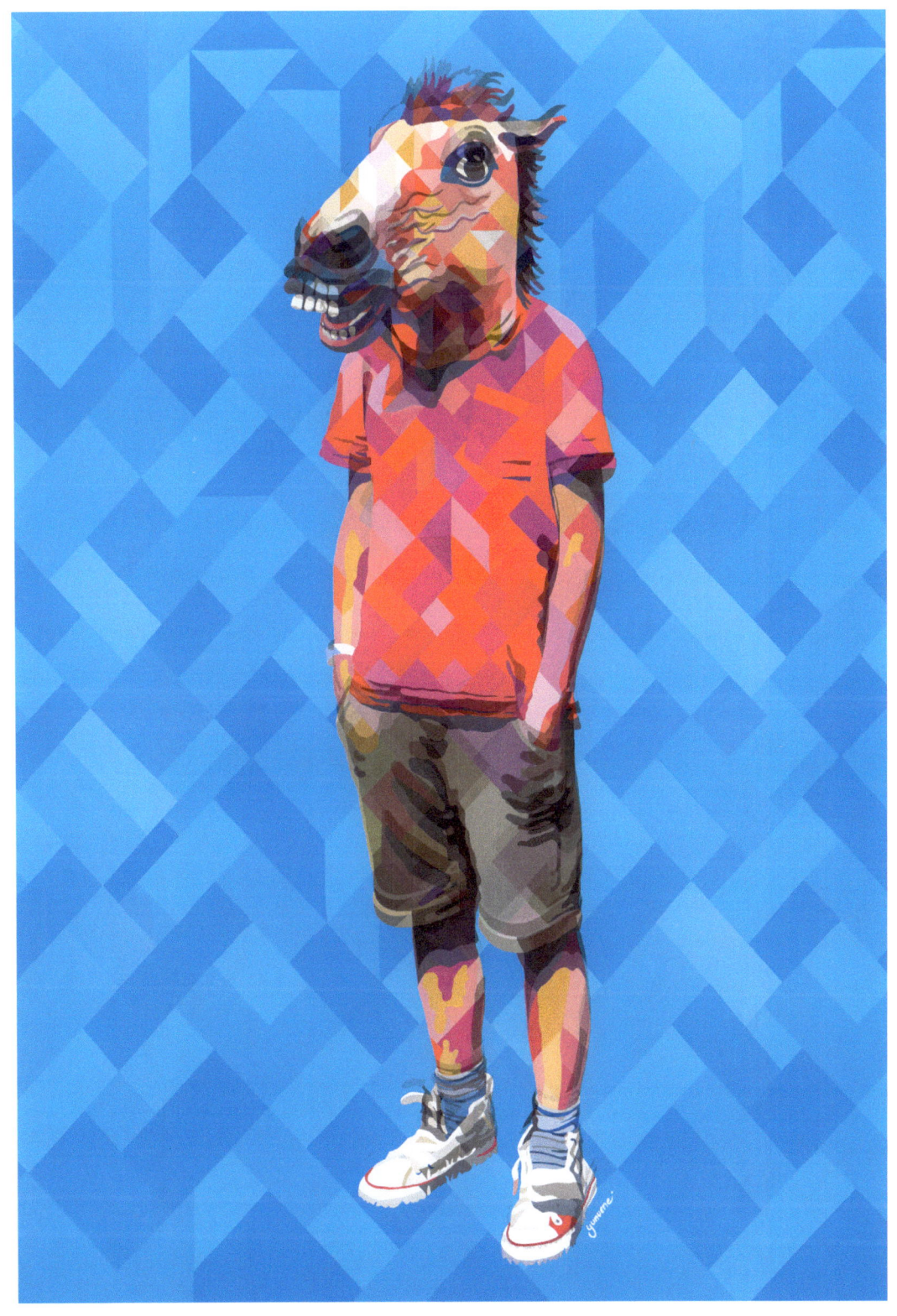

BEAR HUG

2018 / Oil on Canvas / 100x150 cm

Being a mother causes a lot of stress. Life
projects are busted and reinvented,
again and again.

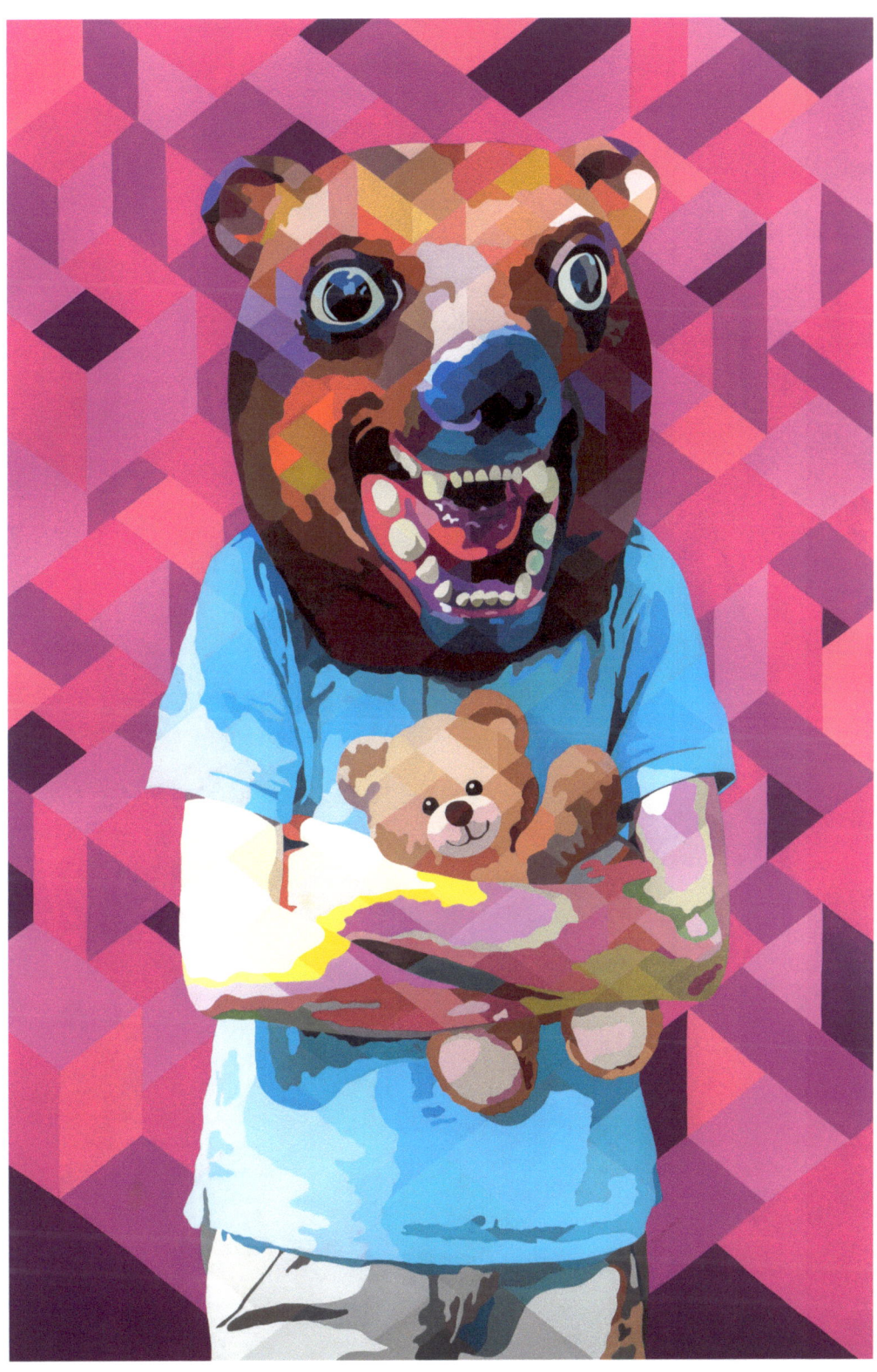

MY WAY OR THE HIGHWAY

2018 / Oil on Canvas / 100x150 cm

As a mother, you learn to go beyond
expectations, and then... you learn to fly.

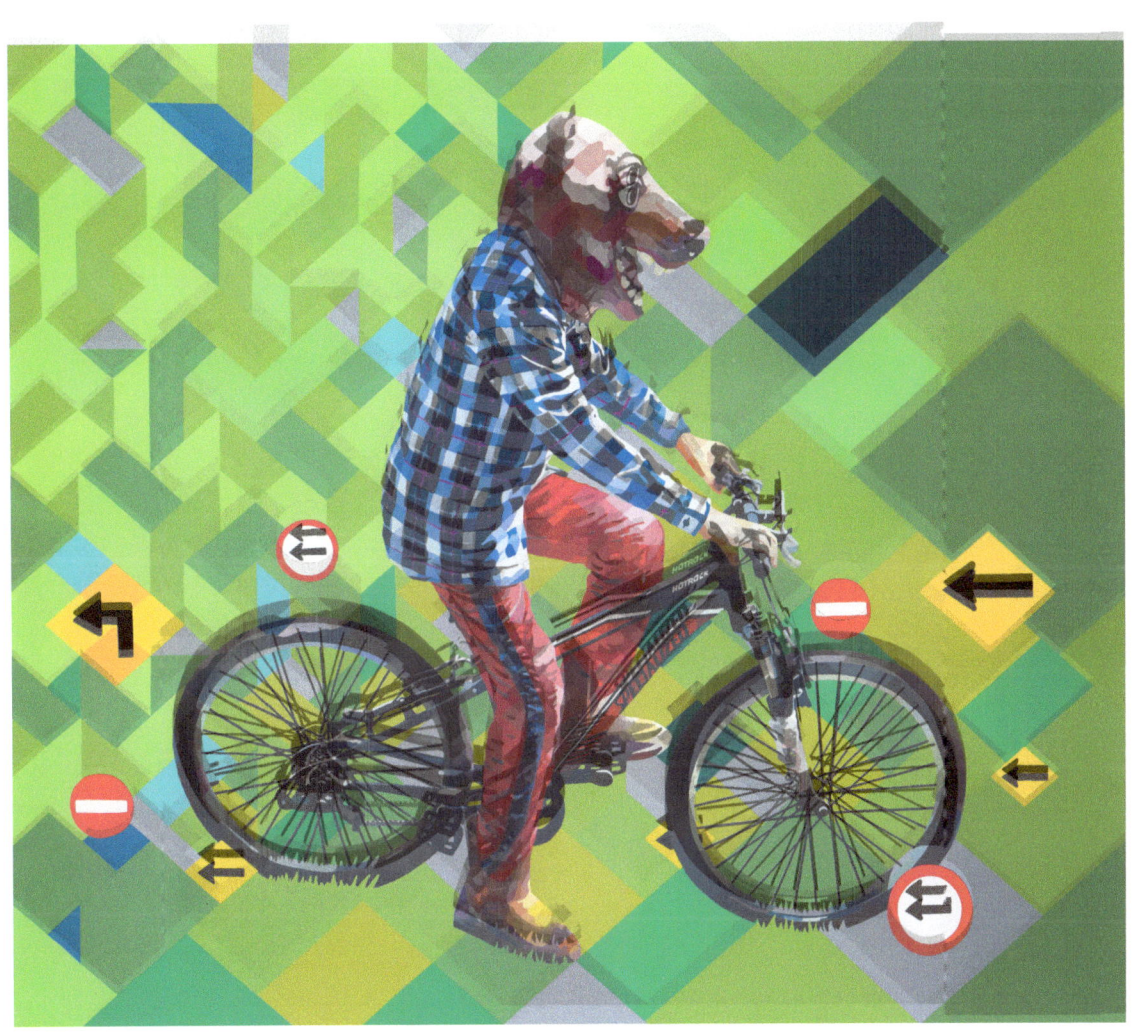

BUBBLE

2019 / Oil on Canvas / 100x150 cm

A mother has a lot in common with a bubble.
Our surface tension keeps us well rounded but
fragile at the same time.

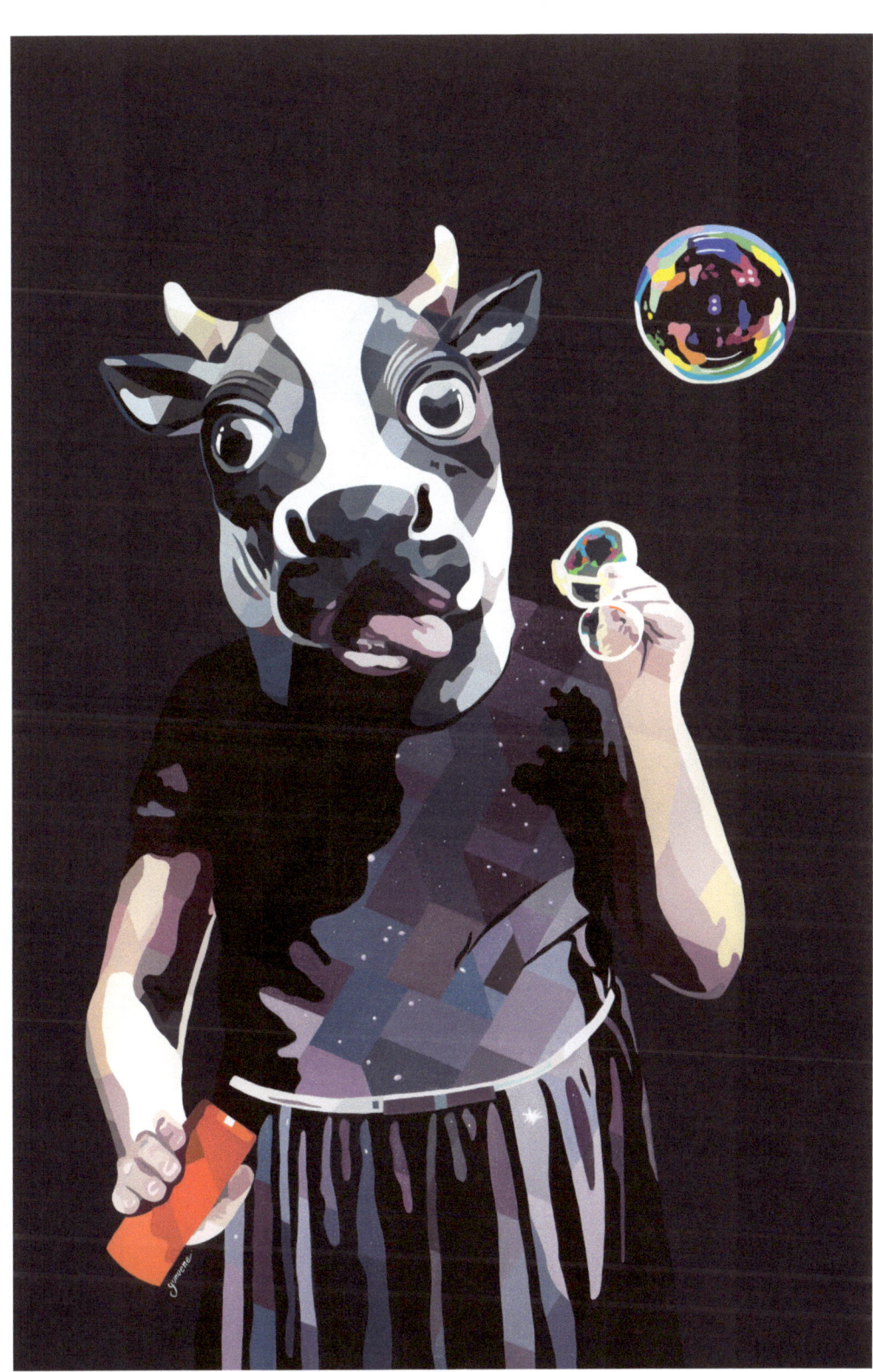

MAGICAL MUSIC SHOW

2018 / Oil on Canvas / 170x200 cm

Motherhood is ordinarily a romantic illusion,
but it becomes a circus surrounded by
surprises, absurdities and contrasts.
It is the rabbit and not the magician
who is in control.

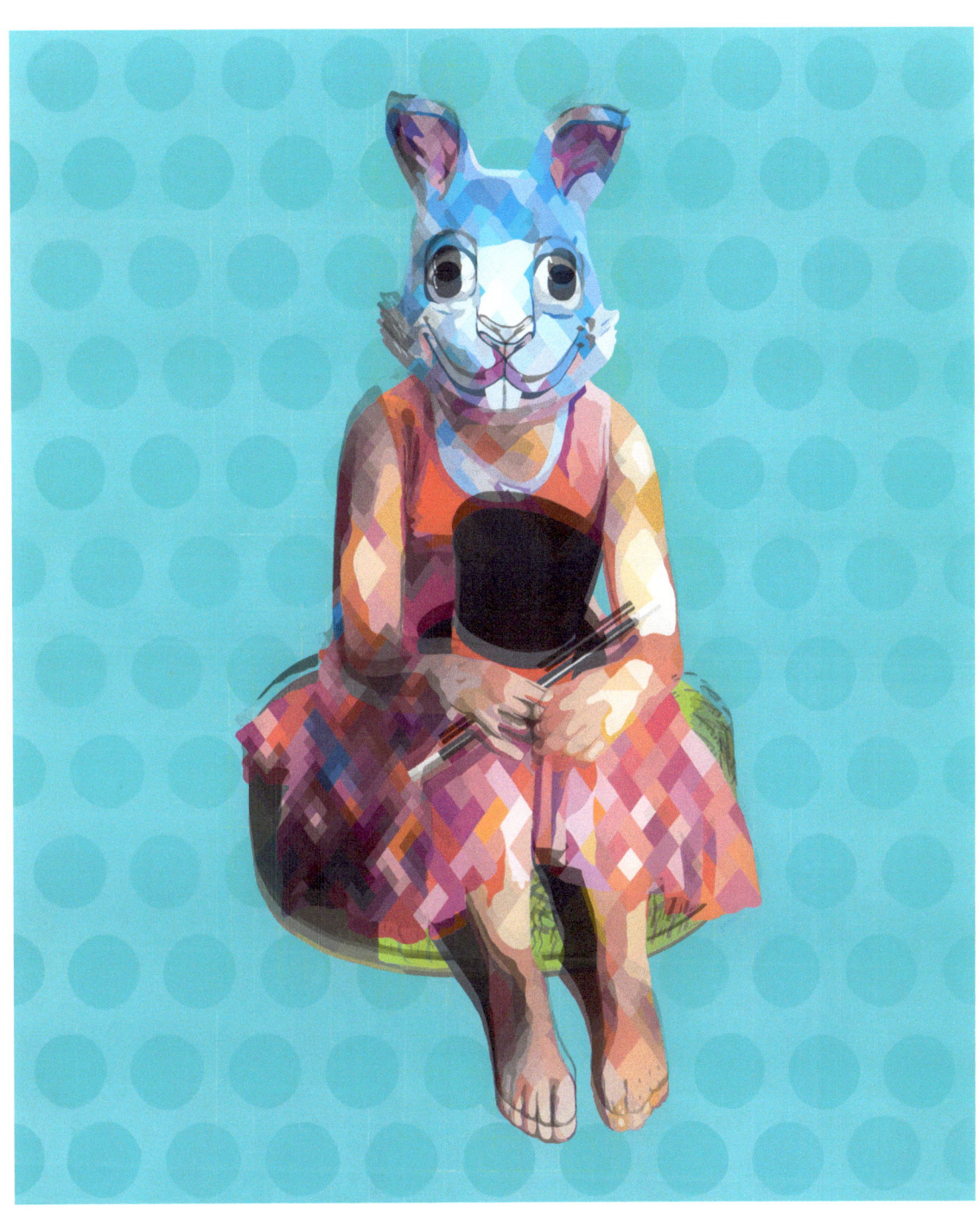

CANNIBAL

2018 / Oil on Canvas / 100x80 cm

Motherhood is letting yourself be devoured in
body and soul to give life to the
next generation.

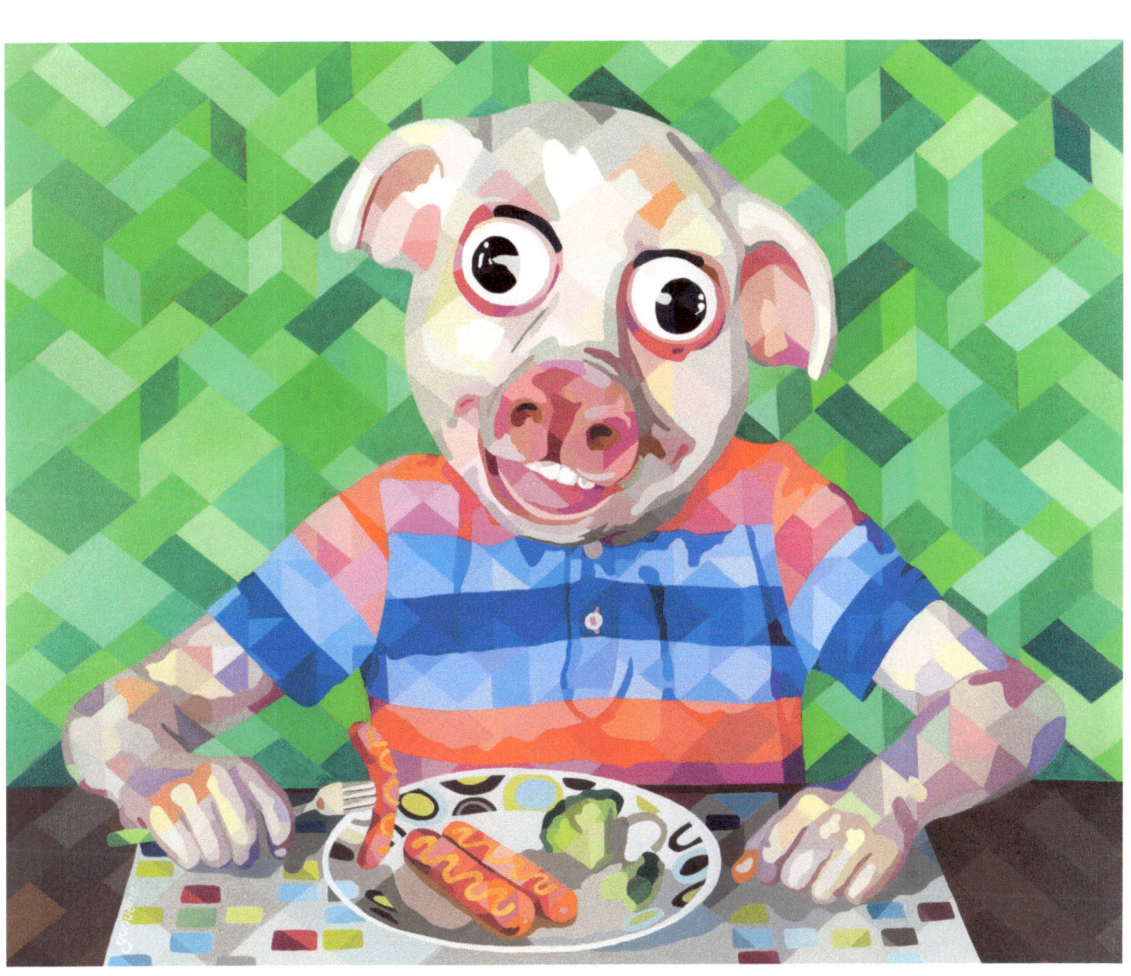

HORSING AROUND

2017 / Oil on Canvas / 90x70 cm

Motherhood is the end of boredom. There is not a moment's rest; instead, life becomes a mysterious formula.

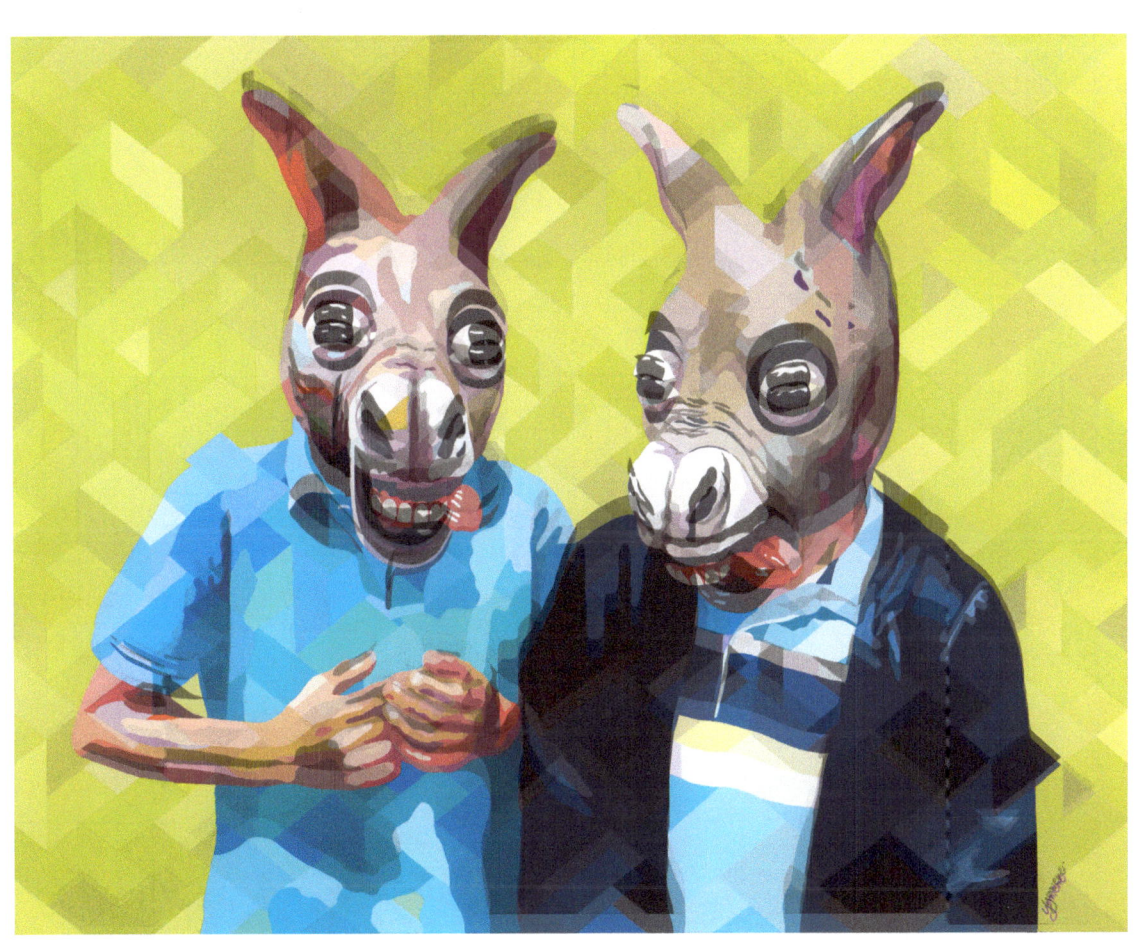

MONKEY BUSINESS

2018 / Oil on Canvas / 90x120 cm

Motherhood is letting go.
Every so often you have to give up control,
think outside the box and trust that
everything will be fine.

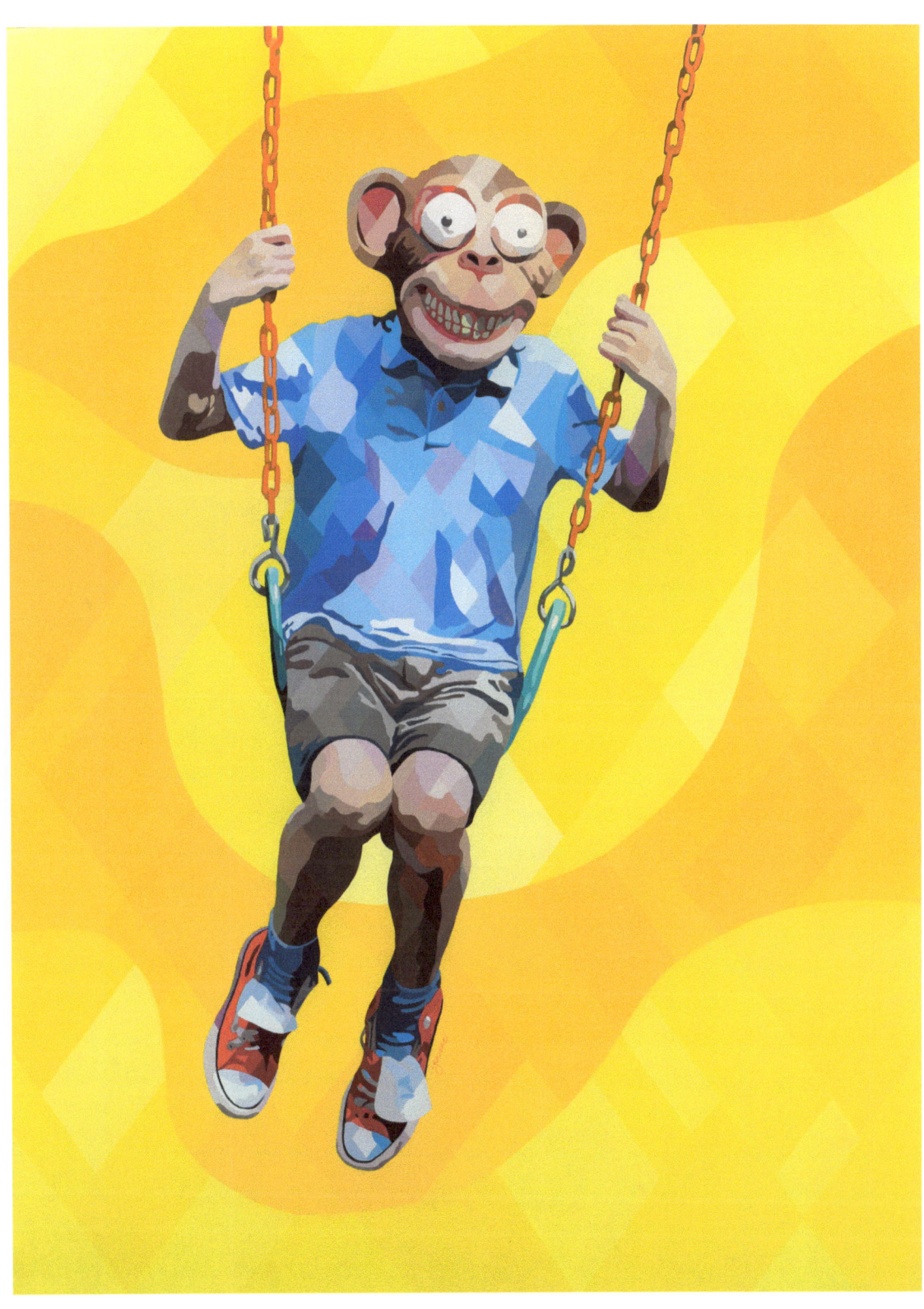

BETWEEN TWO WORLDS
COLLECTION

If you are on people's minds every day, are you alive or dead? Some women transcend death and leave us an exemplary legacy.

MALINCHE

2018 / Oil on Canvas / 70x90 cm

Malintzin, known as Doña Marina in Spain (1500-1551). Mother of Mexican culture.

It was this Nahua woman who constructed a bridge between two civilizations. Victim to some, a traitor to others, but in the end she is recognized as the mother of the base of the mestizo culture of Mexicanness.

Generation after generation, Mexican cultural diversity acquires thousands of shapes and colors.

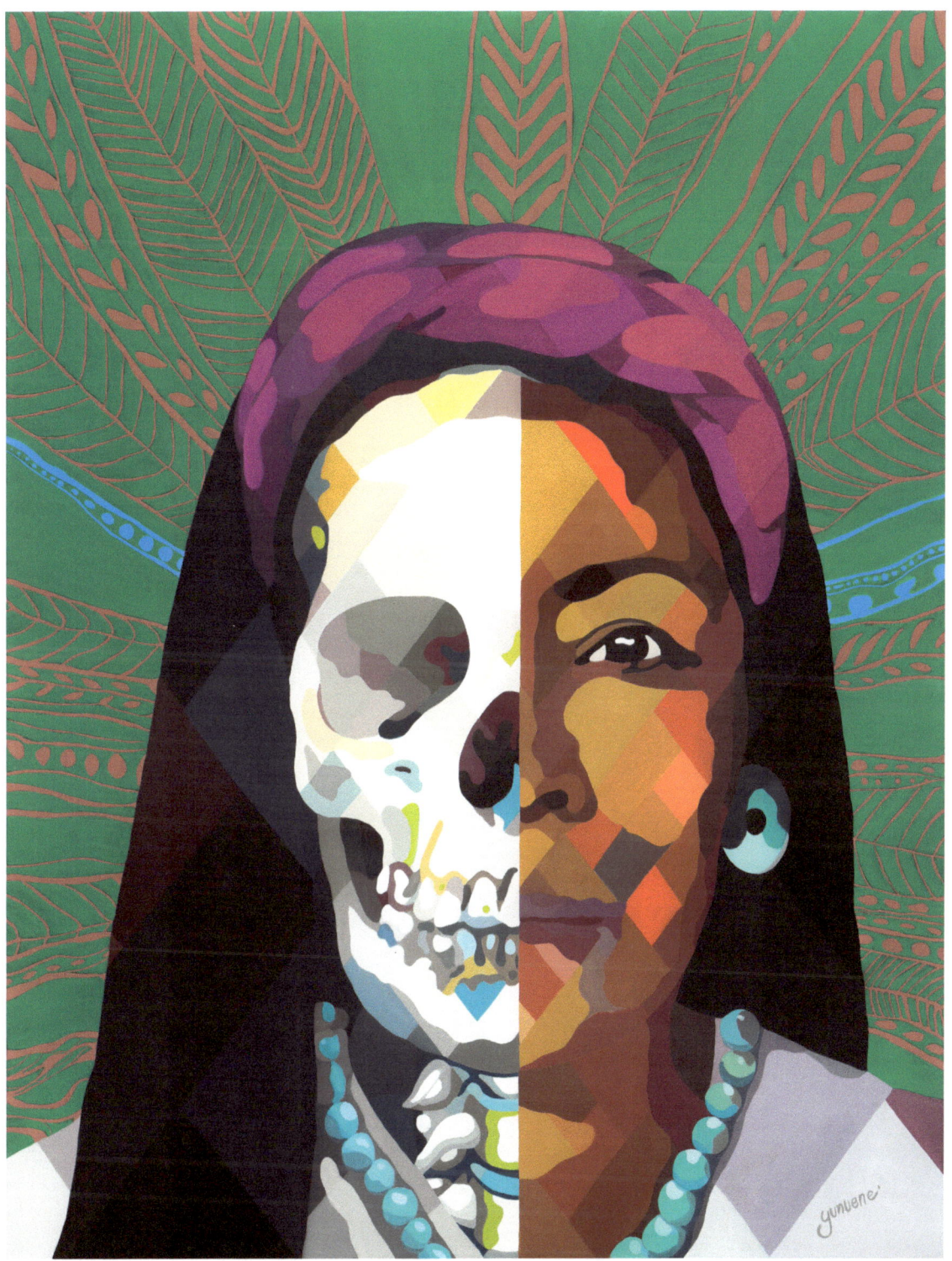

SOR JUANA

2018 / Oil on Canvas / 70x90 cm

Juana Inés de Asbaje and Ramírez de Santillana (1648-1695). Writer from the New Spain.

Called by many the first Mexican feminist for her constant fight for women's right to gain acknowledgment.

She embodied independent and avant-garde thinking in the era of the vice-royalty, in which women had to play a submissive and accessory role. Her literary legacy remains a source of inspiration to this day.

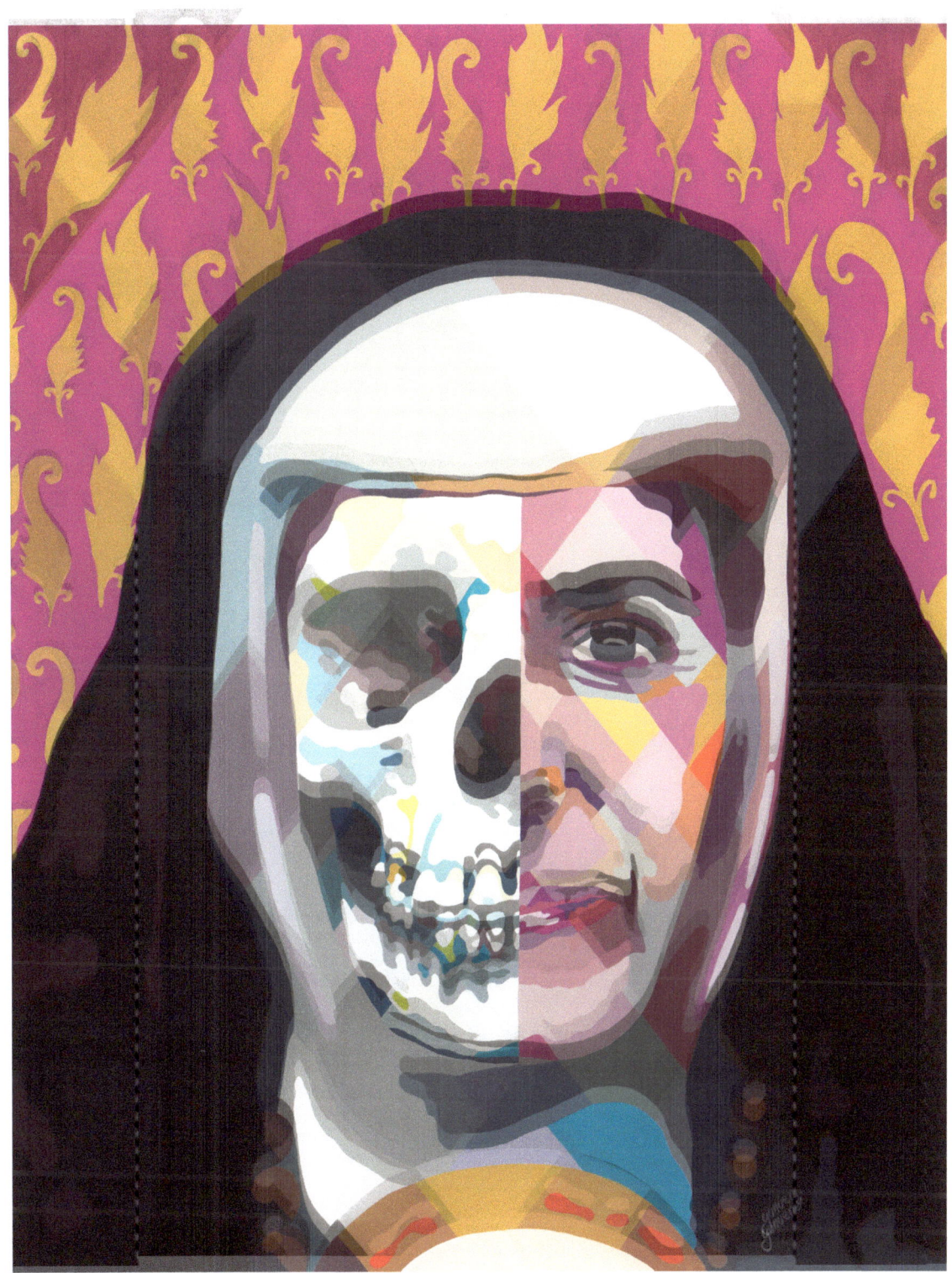

FRIDA

2018 / Oil on Canvas / 70x90 cm

Magdalena Carmen Frida Kahlo Calderón
(1907-1954). Mexican painter.

She took advantage of adversities to leave
a pictorial legacy that reflects an infinite
pain. Art was her unique way of dealing with
suffering. Strength and independence prevail
in each of her works.

She repeatedly showed herself in her paintings
coexisting with both life and death.

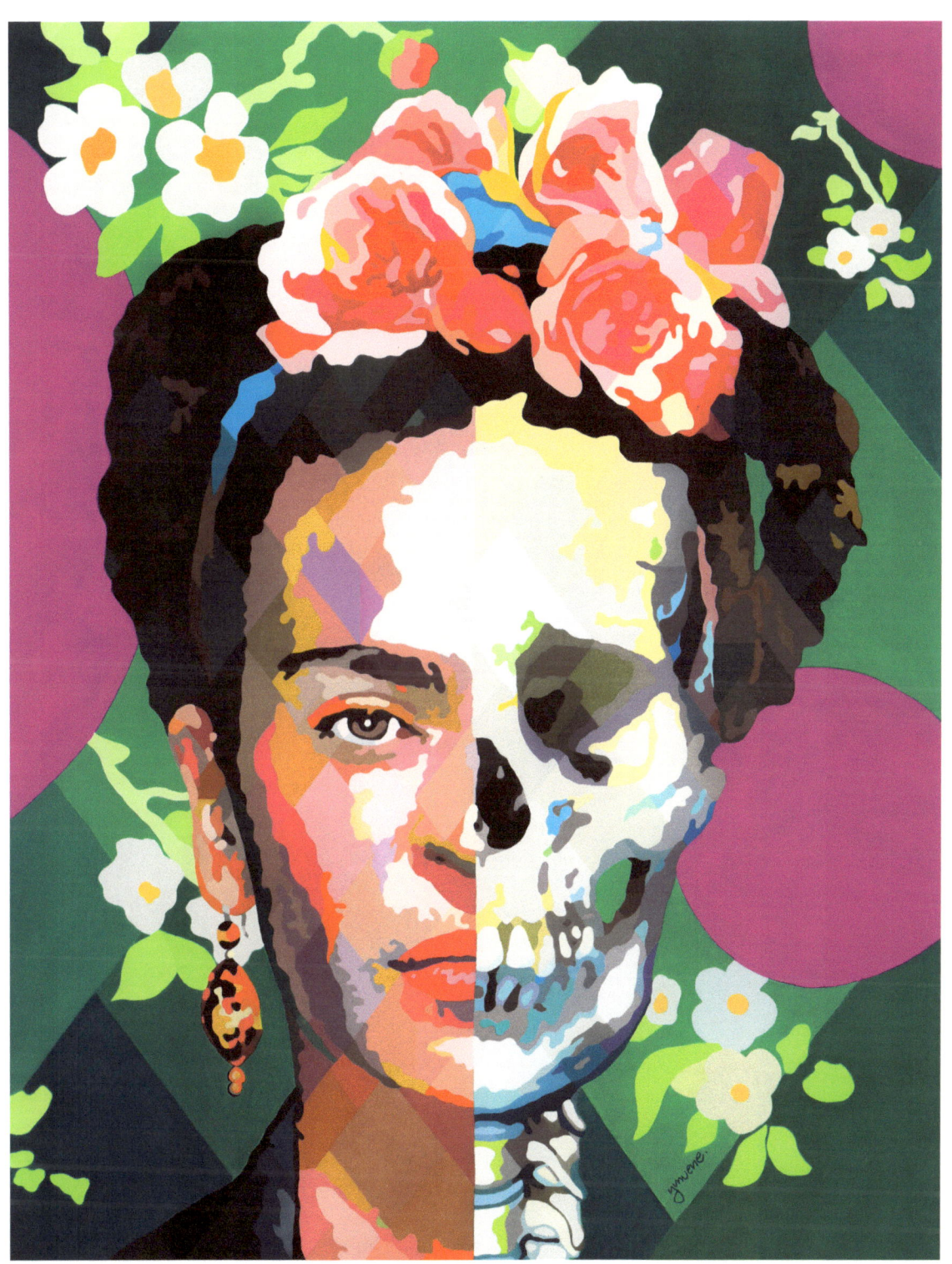

ANONYMOUS

2018 / Oil on Canvas / 70x90 cm

The woman of today.

This work is a tribute to women who have been victims of the gender violence that is motivated by hatred, contempt, or a sense of possession. Women who were deprived of their dreams and goals.
Each one has a story and a name, although it is sometimes unknown.

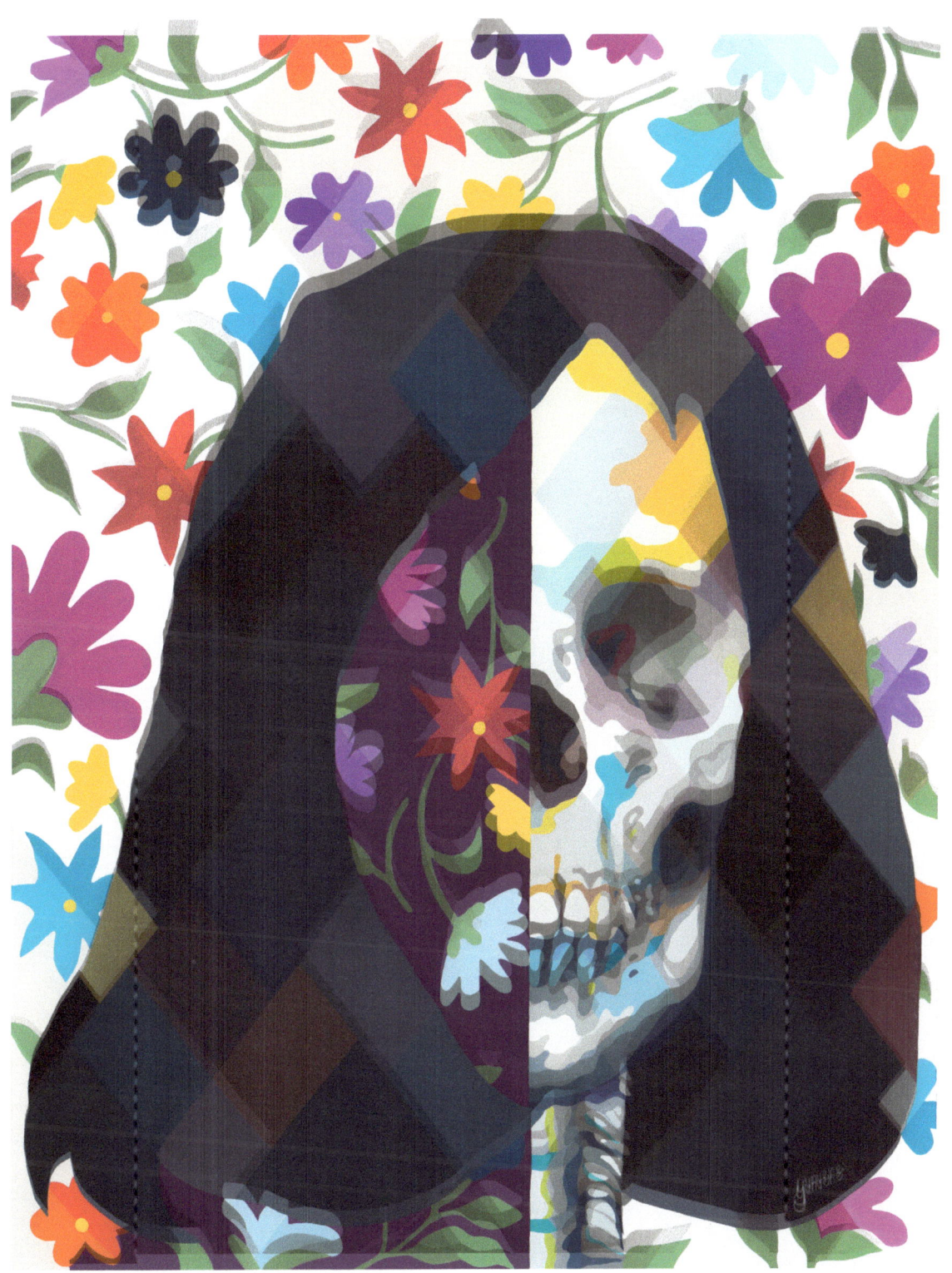

DAILY LIFE 1

COLLECTION

The world around us is a masterpiece...
                       we have only to appreciate it.

MUSICIAN'S SHADOW

2015 / Oil on Canvas / 100x80 cm

Pedro plays the second trumpet, in the back…
Always behind the main act.
All he desired to achieve in life was to
perform. As the notes flow from his lips, he
knows he will never become the first trumpet.

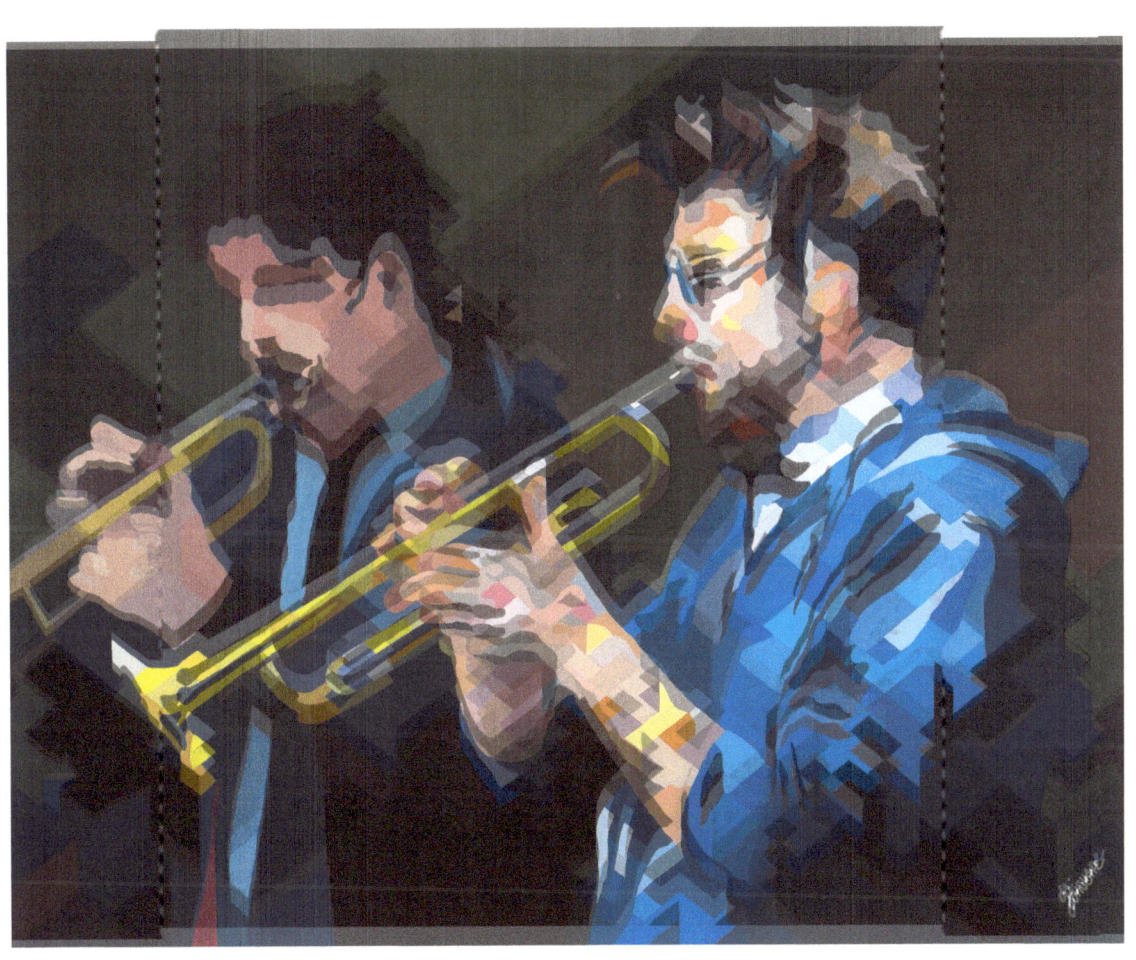

SWIMMING AMONG CLOUDS

2014 / Oil on Canvas / 100x80 cm

When we were children, swimming in the water made us feel capable of flying despite possessing no wings. This child not only swims, but balances the forces of nature.

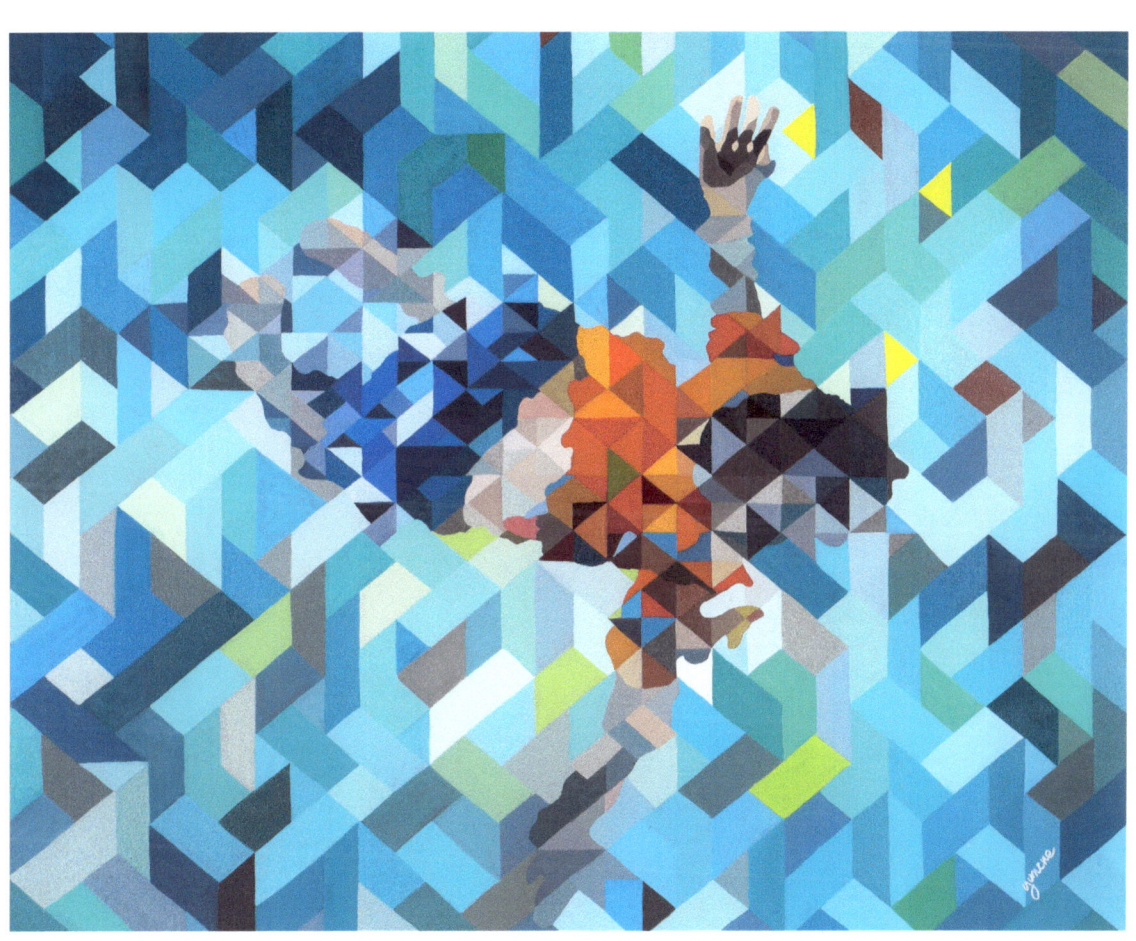

CINDERELLA

2011 / Oil on Canvas / 120x70 cm

These sandals belong to the contemporary woman. She believes that happiness can be achieved in many ways. Not merely by marrying a prince or having a pair of crystal slippers. She doesn't require any help from magical creatures.

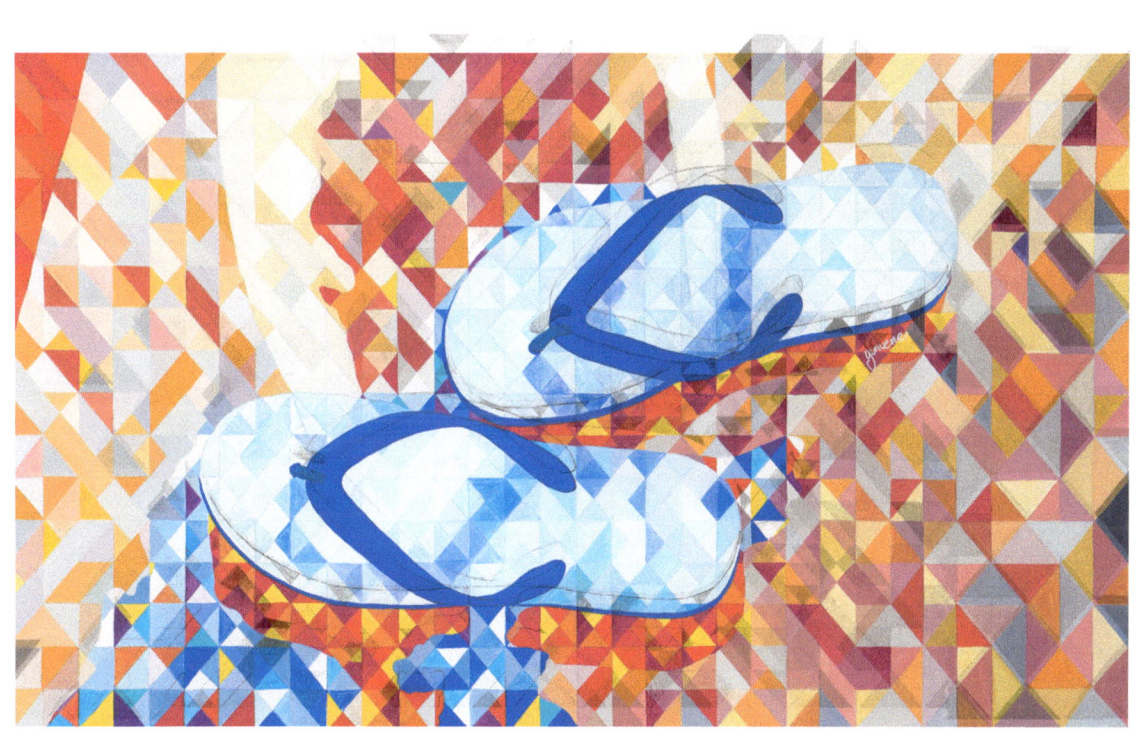

BRIDESMAID

2015 / Oil on Canvas / 70x100 cm

She has served at countless weddings, hoping
one day to attend her own. But fate delivers
other plans as it continues to
shatter her dreams.

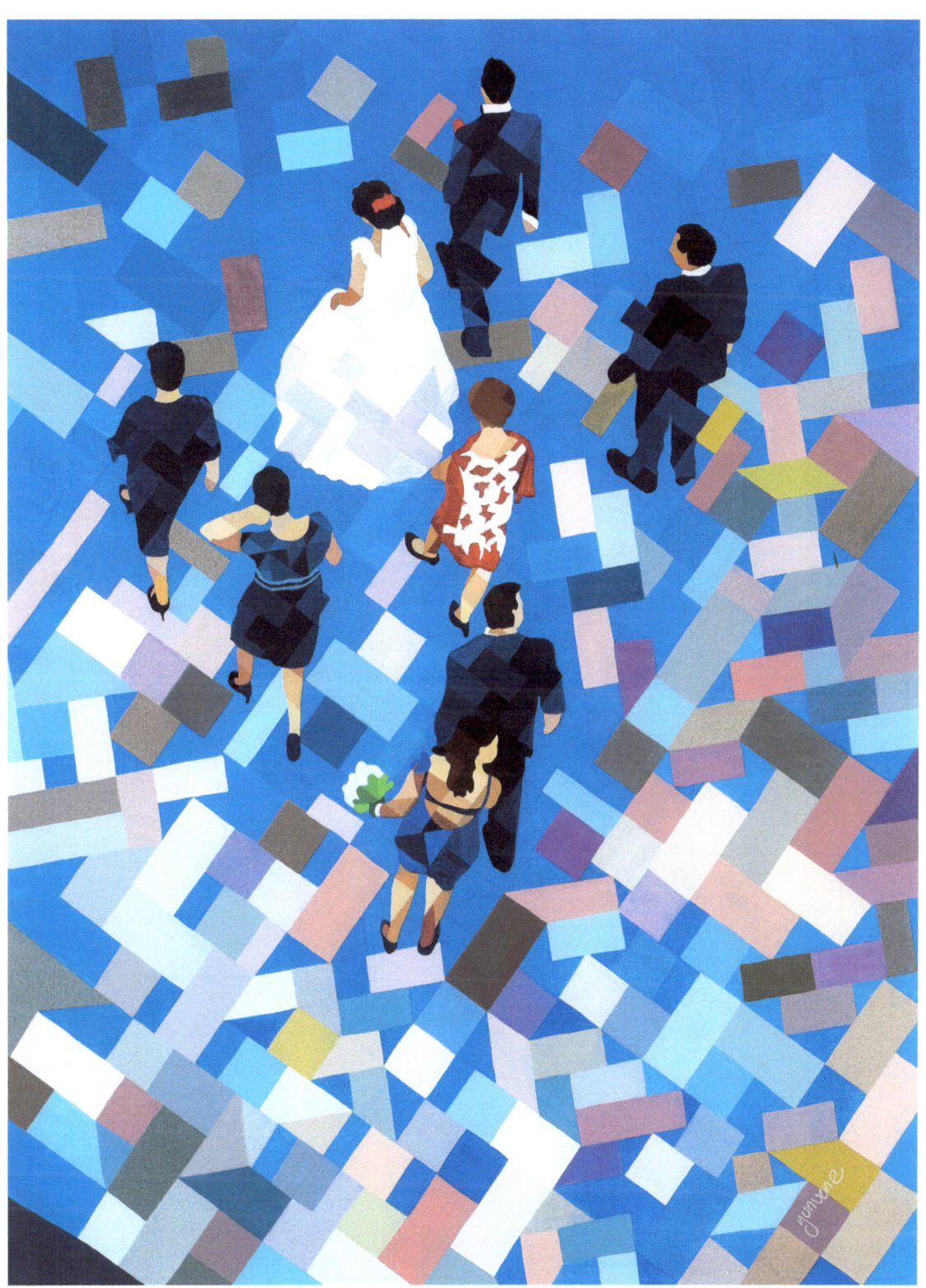

FALL IN THE CITY

2015 / Oil on Canvas / 80x60 cm

Sunset at the park. Tranquility flourishes in every corner. Until we remember we are in Mexico City.

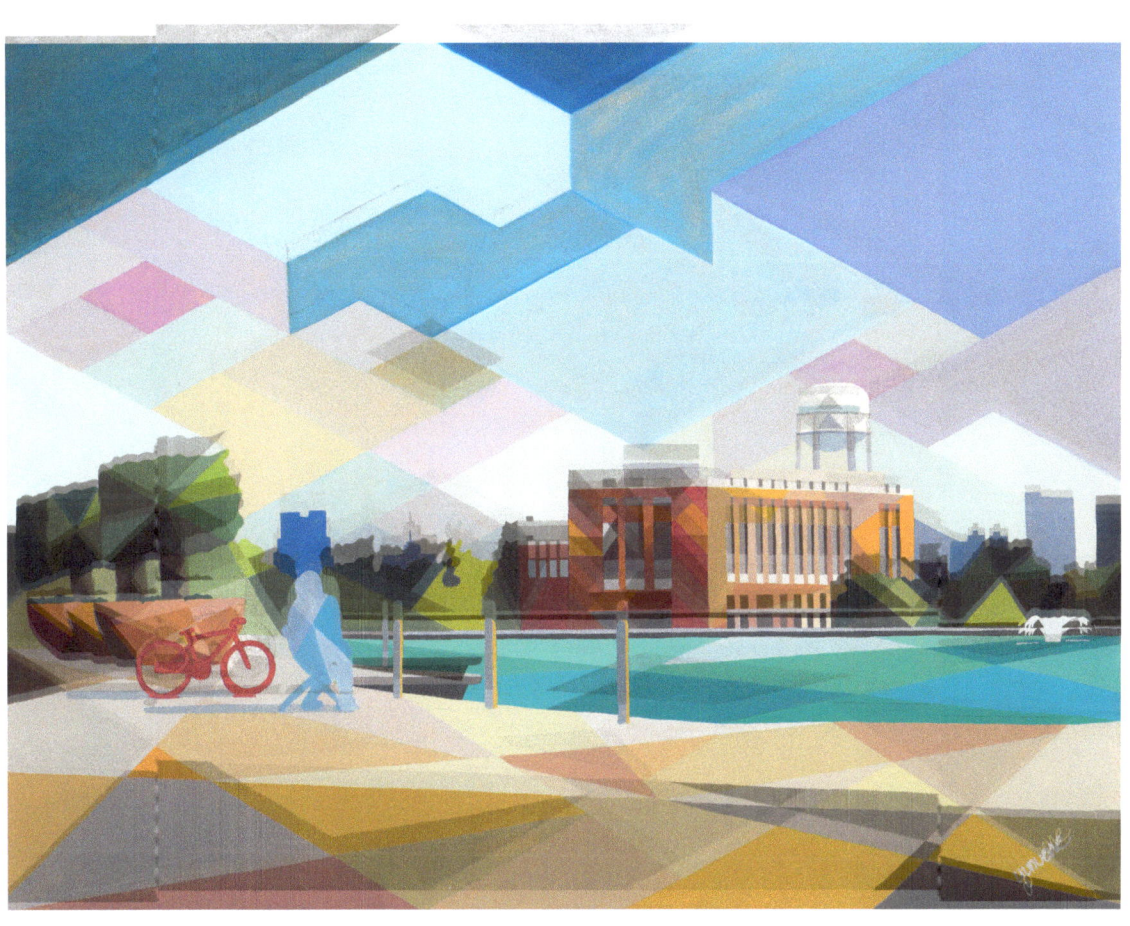

THE FIFTH DOVE

2013 / Oil on Canvas / 70x90 cm

Without warning, the bells began ringing like a call from God, disturbing the peace. At that exact moment, I experienced all my senses awaken. It made me think of the inherent fragility of life. The course of destiny can change from one second to the next.

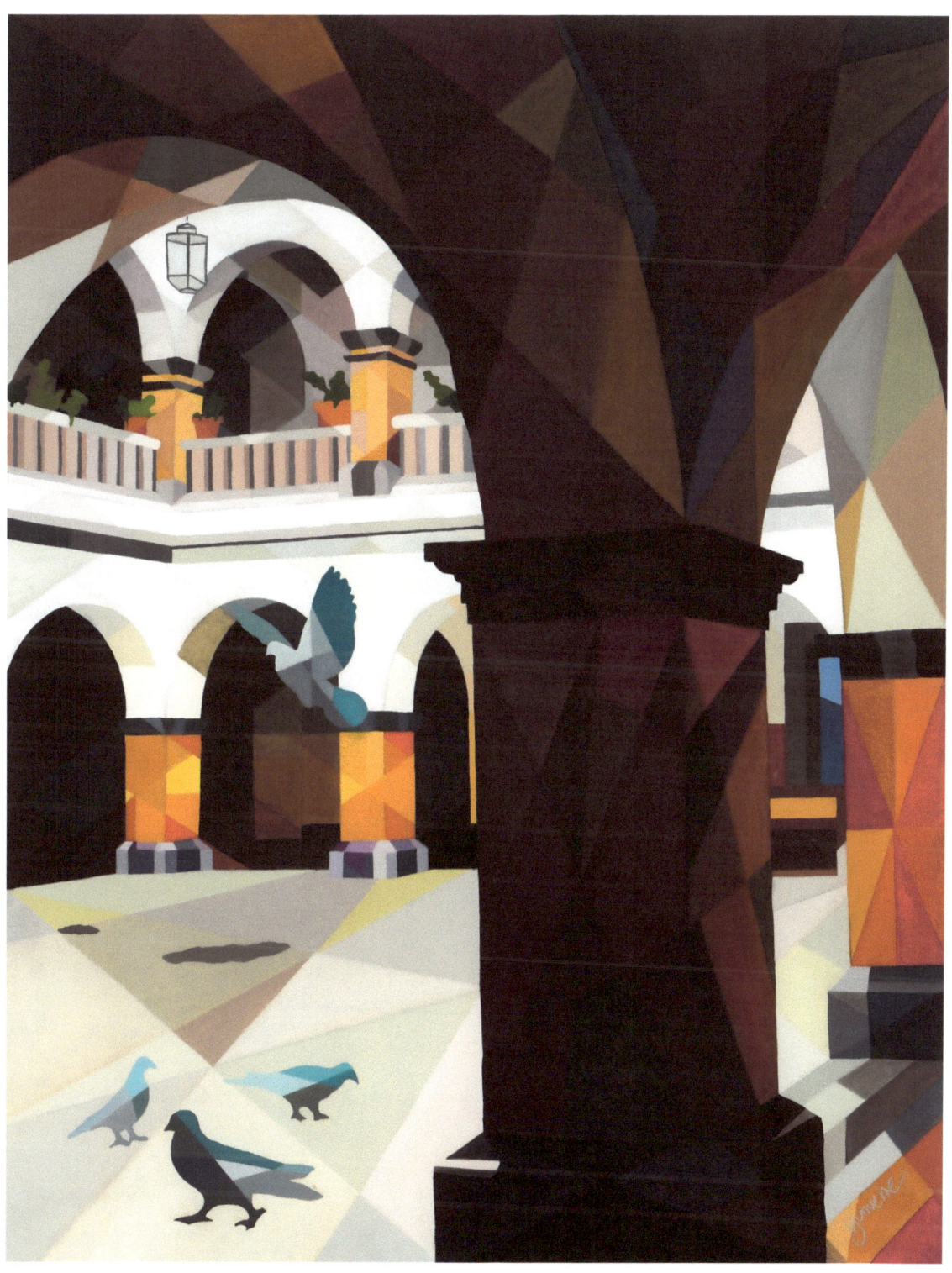

NEVER SAY NEVER
NUNCA DIGAS NUNCA

2015 / Oil on Canvas / 70x90 cm

An abandoned monastery. Some said the faithful would never leave this small town. But time always has a way of showing us that nothing truly lasts forever.

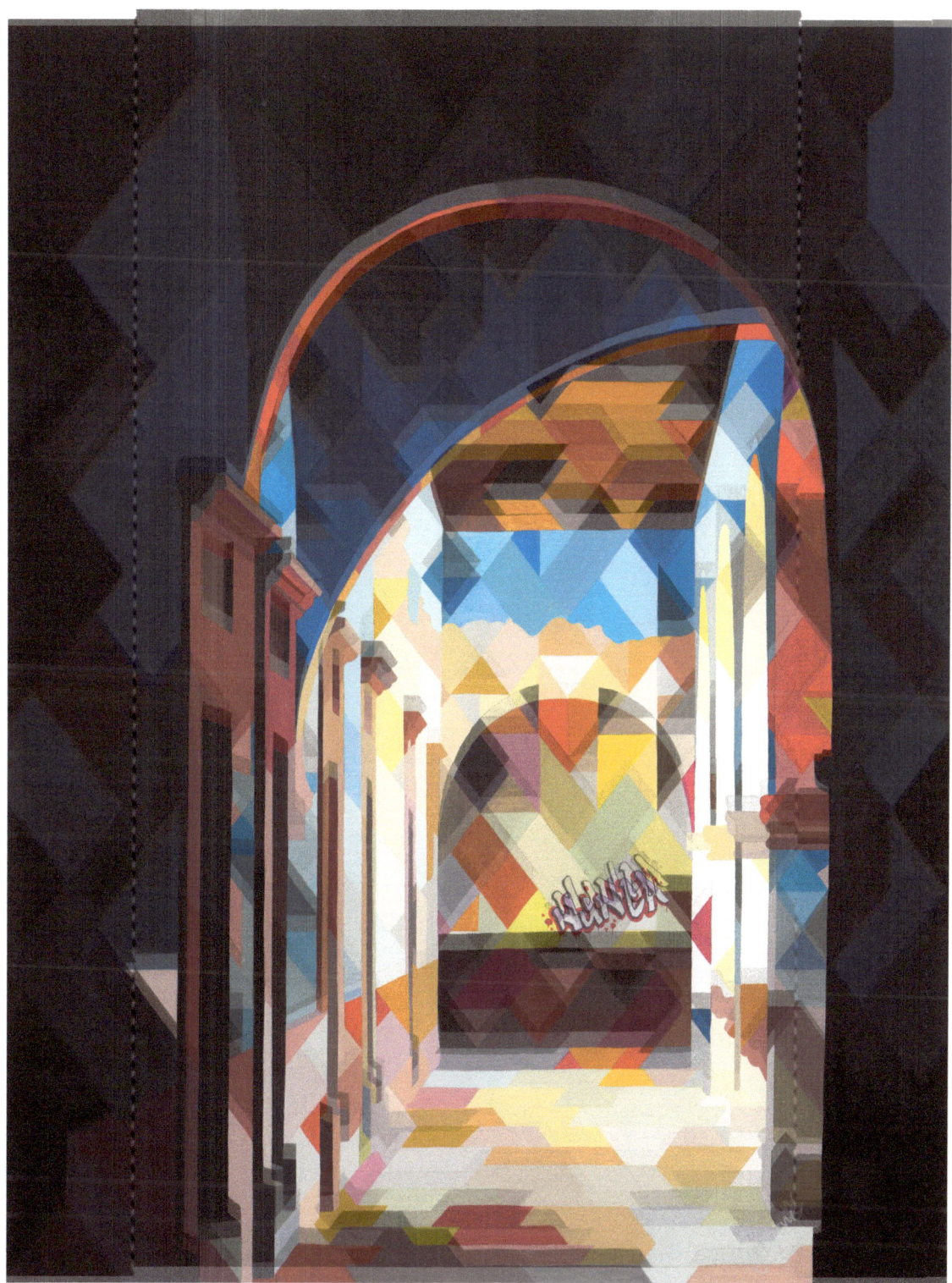

RUBBER PARK

2013 / Oil on Canvas / 70x90 cm

An abandoned industrial park. After many
years of spilling toxic residues into the lake,
local wildlife will never be the same.

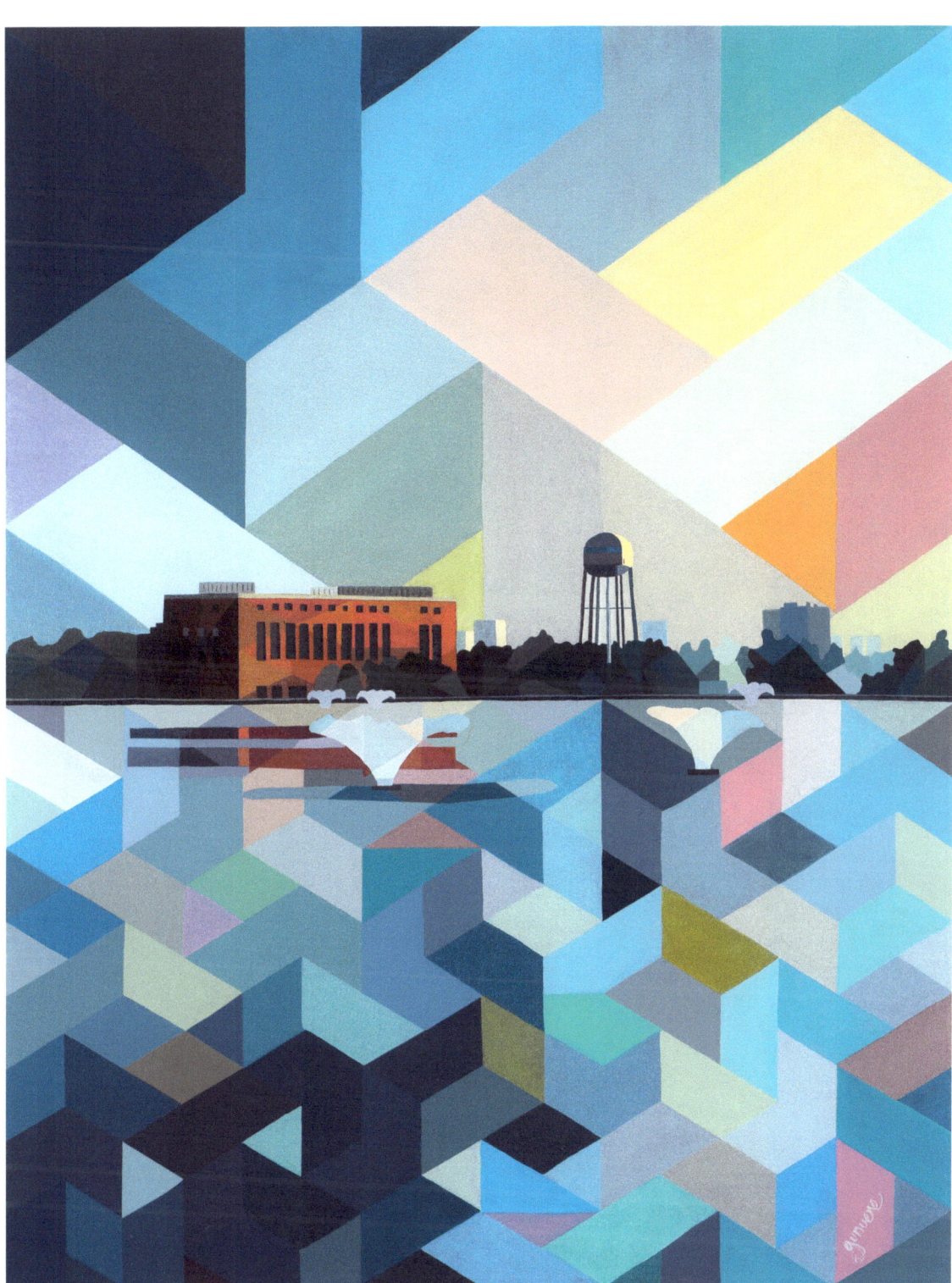

Copyright © 2024 by Yunuen Esparza - YUNUENE

All rights reserved. No part of this publication may be reproduced, distributed, or transmitted in any form or by any means, including photocopying, recording, or other electronic or mechanical methods, without the prior written permission of the publisher, except in the case of brief quotations embodied in critical reviews and certain other non-commercial uses permitted by copyright law. For permission requests, write to the publisher, addressed "Attention: Permissions Coordinator", at the email address: info@yunuene.com

App Store and Apple logo are trademarks of Apple Inc., registered in the U.S. and other countries.
Google Play and the Google Play logo are trademarks of Google LLC.

Compiled, edited and designed by:
José Luis Almeida

Music credits: yunuene.com/credits/

www.yunuene.com

Printed on natural recyclable materials (paper)

First Edition
1 2 3 4 5 6 7 8 9 10

www.ingramcontent.com/pod-product-compliance
Lightning Source LLC
Chambersburg PA
CBHW051922210526
45473CB00006B/2104